HODDER
EDUCATION

The publishers would like to thank the following for permission to reproduce copyright material:

Photo credits: p.50 © Imagestate Media (John Foxx); p.52 © Stockbyte / Alamy

Every effort has been made to trace all copyright holders, but if any have been inadvertently overlooked, the Publishers will be pleased to make the necessary arrangements at the first opportunity.

Although every effort has been made to ensure that website addresses are correct at time of going to press, Hodder Education cannot be held responsible for the content of any website mentioned in this book. It is sometimes possible to find a relocated web page by typing in the address of the home page for a website in the URL window of your browser.

Hachette UK's policy is to use papers that are natural, renewable and recyclable products and made from wood grown in sustainable forests. The logging and manufacturing processes are expected to conform to the environmental regulations of the country of origin.

Orders: please contact Bookpoint Ltd, 130 Milton Park, Abingdon, Oxon OX14 4SB. Telephone: (44) 01235 827720. Fax: (44) 01235 400454. Lines are open 9.00–5.00, Monday to Saturday, with a 24-hour message answering service. Visit our website at www.hoddereducation.co.uk

First published in 2012 by
Hodder Education, a Hachette UK company,
338 Euston Road
London NW1 3BH

Impression number 5 4 3 2 1
Year 2016 2015 2014 2013 2012

Illustrations by Pantek Media, Maidstone, Kent
Typeset in ITC Stone Informal by Pantek Media, Maidstone, Kent
Printed in Spain

A catalogue record for this title is available from the British Library

ISBN 978 1444 156270

Contents

Chapter 4: Circle patterns

Chapter 5: Fitting in

Introduction

These books are intended to help you to make sense of the maths you do in school and the maths you need to use outside school. They have already been tried out in classrooms, and are the result of many comments made by the teachers and the students who have used them. Students told us that after working with these materials they were more able to understand the maths they had done, and teachers found that students also did better in tests and examinations.

Most of the time you will be working 'in context' – in other words, in real-life situations that you will either have been in yourself or can imagine being in. For example, in this book you will be looking at tiling, packing boxes, and pricing stained glass windows, among many other things.

You will regularly be asked to 'draw something' – drawings and sketches are very important in maths and often help us to solve problems and to see connections between different topics. This is particularly true for the work on area and volume.

You will also be expected to talk about your maths, explaining your ideas to small groups or to the whole class. We all learn by explaining our own ideas and by listening to and trying out the ideas of others.

Finally, of course, you will be expected to practice solving problems and answering examination questions.

We hope that through working in this way you will come to understand the maths you do, enjoy examination success, and be confident when using your maths outside school.

A green and pleasant land?

1. Using the map above, estimate the answer to the following questions. Describe how you found each answer.

   a) How many Northern Irelands will fit into Scotland?

   b) How many Northern Irelands will fit into England?

   c) How many Scotlands will fit into England?

2. In 2006 the population of Wales was around 3 million people. Write down what you think were the populations of:

   a) Northern Ireland

   b) Scotland

   c) England

3. How do your estimates compare with the actual population figures?

4. How can you explain any differences?

The delivery driver

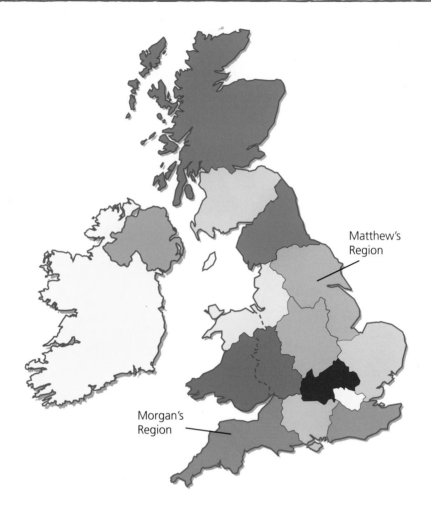

Matthew's Region

Morgan's Region

5 Digital Deliveries Limited is a company that deals in electronic equipment in the UK.

The map above shows the delivery regions for this company.

In which type of region would you prefer to be a van driver? Explain.

6 Matthew covers the Yorkshire and Lincolnshire region. He claims that he has a bigger region to cover than Morgan, who drives in the South West region. Which region do you think is bigger? Explain your reasoning.

7 See if you can identify other pairs of regions that are roughly the same size.

Pricing tiles

8 Here is a design for an arrangement of tiles that could be used in the home or garden:

The price of a standard-sized tile as shown by the arrow is £1.80.

Work out fair prices for the other tiles in this design.

There is a copy of this picture in **Workbook exercise 1.1** (on page 1 of your workbook) which you can use to answer this question.

Discuss your strategies with your classmates.

 Turn to pages 1–3 in your workbook and do the other questions in Workbook exercise 1.1.

Stained glass

9 Stained glass windows have been popular in churches and houses since the 11th century. Some designs from the 19th and 20th centuries are still used today.

    a) When was the house or flat that you live in built? Does it have any stained glass?

    b) What about your school building?

    c) Where was the last place you saw stained glass?

10 Look at the pictures below. Think about any stained glass windows you have seen. What sorts of shapes are popular for stained glass windows? Sketch and name some examples of shapes used in stained glass windows.

1920s house

1890s house

11 A company uses rectangular sheets of coloured glass. They cut pieces from these to make a window.

Each rectangular sheet measures 6 inches by 4 inches and costs £18.

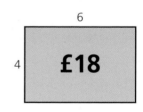

Work out the cost of each piece of coloured glass.

a)
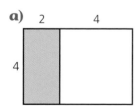

b)
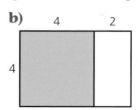

c)
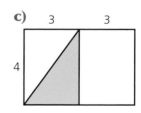

 Now try Workbook exercises 1.2, 1.3 and 1.4 (pages 4–6) in your workbook.

Cleaning windows

12 Chris and Alex work for a window cleaning firm. They specialise in cleaning high-rise buildings. They charge by the pane of glass.

How many windows can you see in the hotel building pictured below? Compare your method of counting with your neighbour's.

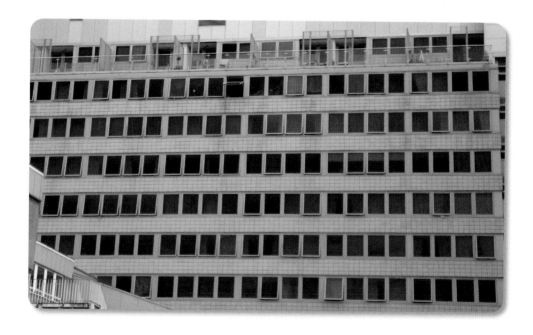

 Turn to pages 7–8 in your workbook and try Workbook exercise 1.5.

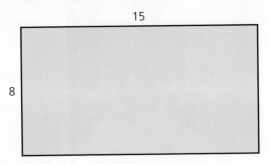

Class activity 1

Touching the numbers: The rectangle

Look at the rectangle above.
- Where do you see a distance of 15 in this picture? Run your finger along exactly where you see the distance of 15.
- Where else can you see a distance of 15? Again, run your finger along.
- How many places can you see a distance of 15? Run your finger along these too.

Now look at the 8.
- Where do you see a distance of 8 in this picture?
- Where else do you see a distance of 8?
- How many places can you see a distance of 8? Run your finger along all of these.

What is the area of this rectangle?

Where can you see the 120 squares in this picture?

 Turn to pages 9–11 in your workbook and try Workbook exercise 1.6.

Touching the numbers: The trapezium

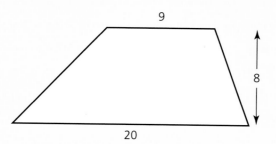

Look at the trapezium above.
- Where do you see a distance of 20 in this picture?
- Where else can you see a distance of 20?
- Where else can you see a distance of 20?
- Run your finger along all the places you can see a distance of 20.

Look at the 8.
- Where do you see a distance of 8?
- Where else can you see a distance of 8?
- Where else can you see a distance of 8?
- Again, run your finger along all the places you can see a distance of 8.

Look at the 9.
- Where do you see a distance of 9?
- Where else can you see a distance of 9?
- Where else can you see a distance of 9?
- Run your finger along all the places you can see a distance of 9.

Where can you see a distance of 11 in this picture?
- Run your finger along all the places you can see a distance of 11.

13 Try to find the area of this shape.

14 Below is Tom's attempt to answer this question. Describe what you think Tom has done.

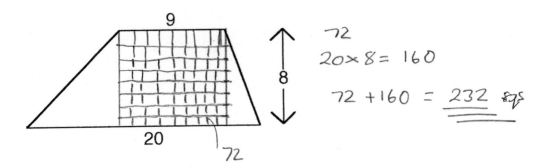

$$72$$
$$20 \times 8 = 160$$
$$72 + 160 = \underline{232} \text{ sqs}$$

15 Below is Sandra's attempt to answer the question. Describe what you think Sandra has done.

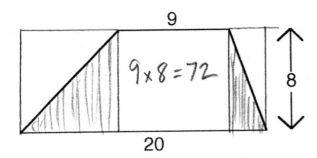

$$9 \times 8 = 72$$

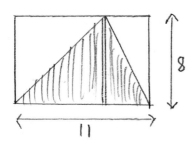

$$8 \times 11 = 88$$
$$88 \div 2 = 44$$
$$72 + 44 = 116 \text{ squares}$$

16 Whose method (if any) do you agree with?

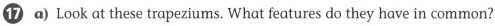

17   **a)** Look at these trapeziums. What features do they have in common?
     b) Find the area of each one.

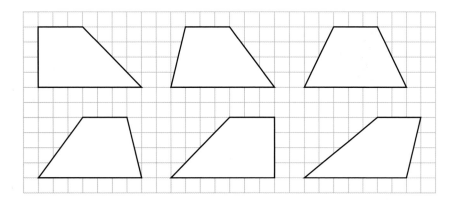

Playground surfaces

18 Look at the picture below.

    a) What do you think the surface of the playground is made of?

    b) Have you ever fallen over in a playground? What type of surface did you land on?

19 Helen and Nigel work for the council. Their job is to work out the cost of surfacing playgrounds.

Below is a possible design for a new playground to be built close to the city centre.

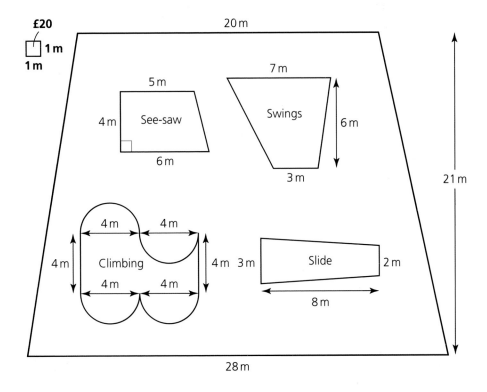

The cheapest cost they can find for a 'spongy' tarmac is £20 for a square metre.

a) Make a tracing of the outline of the playground.

b) Experiment with ways of working out the cost of surfacing the whole area in 'spongy' tarmac. Try a few ways of doing this.

Sometimes it is cheaper to use 'spongy' tarmac just for the areas below the equipment and hard tarmac in between. Helen and Nigel investigate the cost of this. These areas can be seen in your workbook in **Workbook exercise 1.7**.

 Turn to pages 12–14 in your workbook and try Workbook exercise 1.7.

Summary

In this chapter you looked at ways of finding the area of various shapes:

By 'realloting' parts of the shape.

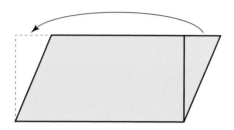

By creating a surrounding rectangle.

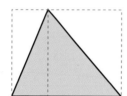 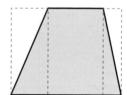

By seeing how many squares you could fit into each shape.

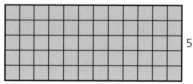

Triangle types

1 A list of types of triangle is given here:

Angle properties	Side properties
Obtuse-angled triangle	Scalene triangle
Acute-angled triangle	Isosceles triangle
Right-angled triangle	Equilateral triangle

a) In pairs, draw an example of each of the above types of triangle.

b) Can a triangle have more than one of the properties above?

2 List the properties (for example, obtuse-angled triangle, equilateral triangle, and so on) of each of the triangles below. You may need a ruler or angle measurer to check whether you are correct.

a)

b)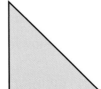

c)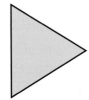

d)

e)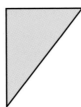

f)

3 You will need a set of narrow straws or pieces of spaghetti of length: 6 cm, 6 cm, 8 cm, 8 cm, 8 cm, 10 cm, 12 cm and 14 cm.

a) Using the straws/spaghetti pieces, can you make:

- a scalene triangle
- a scalene triangle that is also acute
- an isosceles triangle that is also right-angled
- a right-angled triangle that is equilateral
- an obtuse-angled triangle that is isosceles?

b) Is it always possible to make a triangle with three straws/spaghetti pieces?

4 Using the closed loop of string provided, make the following triangles:
- equilateral
- isosceles
- right-angled
- scalene

5 Sometimes you can tell what property a triangle has just by looking at the angles, or just by looking at the lengths of the sides.

What kind of triangles are the following (*hint*: If you are stuck, it may help to draw the triangle):

a) a triangle with angles 60°, 60° and 60°

b) a triangle with two equal angles

c) a triangle with sides of length 3 cm, 4 cm and 5 cm

d) a triangle with sides of length 3 cm, 4 cm and 6 cm

e) a triangle with two angles of 35°

f) a triangle with two angles equal to 45°?

> Information about a triangle in one form often allows you to work out other things about the triangle.

6 The triangle in the diagram below has points A and B fixed where they are on the bottom line. Point C is allowed to move anywhere along the parallel line P.

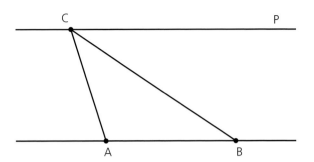

 There is a copy of this diagram which you can use to answer **question 6** on page 15 of your workbook (Workbook exercise 2.1).

Mark the points on line P where:
- ABC is a right-angled triangle (call this/these point(s) C_1)
- ABC is an acute-angled isosceles triangle (call this/these C_2)
- ABC is acute but not isosceles (call this/these C_3)
- ABC is isosceles and obtuse (call this/these C_4)
- ABC is scalene (call this/these C_5)

7 a) Copy the sentence below and fill in the missing word with **smallest, largest** or **pointiest**:

To identify whether a triangle is obtuse, acute or right-angled you need to look at the _____ angle in the triangle.

b) Is it true that the largest angle in a triangle is opposite the largest side?

Making triangles using three squares

8 You will need six sheets of 1 cm² A4 paper, a ruler and some scissors.

9 Carefully draw two squares each with sides of: 2 cm, 3 cm, 4 cm, 5 cm, 6 cm, 8 cm, 10 cm, 12 cm, 13 cm and 15 cm. You will end up with 20 squares.

10 Now write inside each square the area of the square in square centimetres.

11 Carefully cut out the 20 squares.

12 **a)** Now take three of the squares and use them to make a triangle.

b) Here, we have used squares of area 16, 25 and 36 to make a triangle where the largest angle is an acute angle. This is an **acute-angled triangle**.

Make a note of the area of each square and the type of triangle formed (acute-angled triangle, right-angled triangle or obtuse-angled triangle, depending on the size of the largest angle). Record the information in a table like this one:

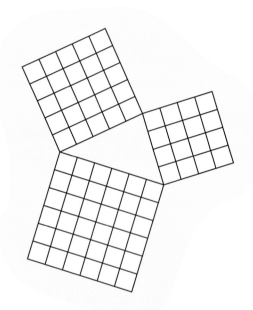

Area of small square (1)	Area of small square (2)	Area of biggest square	Type of triangle (acute/right/obtuse)
16 cm²	25 cm²	36 cm²	Acute

There is a blank table you can use to answer **question 12b)** on page 16 of your workbook (Workbook exercise 2.2).

13 Now pick three more squares and form another triangle. Record the result in the table in your workbook. Repeat this at least six times.

14 Collect the results from the rest of your class.

15 What do you notice about the squares used to make each type of triangle:

    a) acute-angled

    b) right-angled

    c) obtuse-angled?

16 Adam always starts by doing the two shorter sides of the triangle first. For one of his triangles he begins with these two squares.

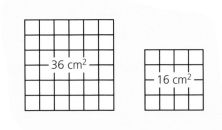

    a) If Adam wants to make an acute-angled triangle, what size square could he use for the longest side of the triangle?

    b) If Adam wants to make an obtuse-angled triangle, what size square could he use for the longest side of the triangle?

17 You are given squares with areas of $4\,cm^2$, $9\,cm^2$ and $16\,cm^2$. What type of triangle would you make? How do you know?

18 You are given squares with areas of $25\,cm^2$, $144\,cm^2$ and $169\,cm^2$. What type of triangle would you make? How do you know?

19 You are given squares with areas of $20\,cm^2$, $30\,cm^2$ and $40\,cm^2$. What type of triangle would you make? How do you know?

20 You are given squares with areas of $23\,cm^2$ and $45\,cm^2$. What size square would you need to make a right-angled triangle?

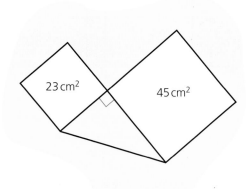

Triangles with a right angle

21 You may already have made this triangle using squares with areas of $9\,cm^2$, $16\,cm^2$ and $25\,cm^2$.

What are the lengths of the sides of the squares shown below?

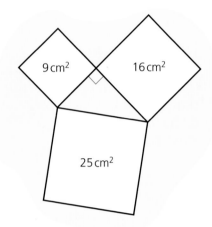

22 What is the connection between the length of the sides of a square and the area (number of squares inside it)?

23 Here is another set of squares that make a right-angled triangle.

What are the lengths of the sides of the squares shown below?

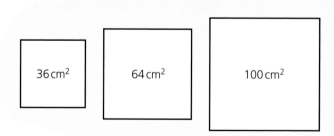

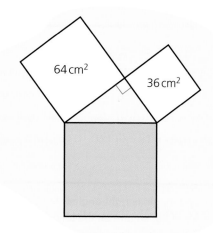

24 What is the area of the green square in this diagram?

25 What is the length of the sides of the green square?

26 Some squares have areas and sides that are whole numbers. For example, a square of area 36 cm² has sides of length 6 cm.

   a) What is the length of the sides of a square with area 49 cm²?

   b) Which other areas of squares have sides that are whole numbers?

   c) What if the area of the square was 42 cm²? Estimate the length of the sides.

27 The actual side length of a square of area 42 cm² is about 6.48 cm. We can find it on a calculator by using the **square root** button.

$$\sqrt{42} = 6.48$$

Try to get this answer on your calculator.

28 Use your calculator to find the square root of:

   a) 90

   b) 68

   c) 20

   d) 1.44

Pythagoras

29 People in ancient civilisations knew about the relationship between the sides and the angles in a triangle. They used this information to construct right angles.

a) Why is it important in buildings to have right angles?

b) Look around you and write down three places where you can see a right angle.

> If a triangle is right-angled, then the area of the square on the longest side is the same as the sum of the areas of the squares on the other two sides.

30 A Greek mathematician called Pythagoras wrote down the relationship between the sides and the angles in a triangle. This is shown in the box above.

Use this idea to work out the area of the largest square in the drawing below.

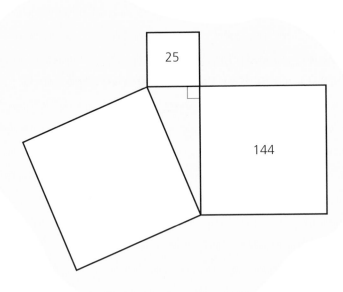

31 Luke used Pythagoras' idea for the drawing on the right. He wanted to find the area of the purple square. He added the areas of the two white squares together and got 136.

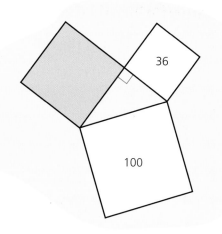

a) Explain why Luke's answer of 136 must be wrong.

b) What is the area of the purple square?

32 Pythagoras realised that if he knew the area of the square, he could work out the length of the side of the triangle. For example, a square of area 64 cm² has sides of 8 cm.

What would be the length of the sides if a square had an area of:

a) 36 cm²

b) 144 cm²?

33 Work out the length of the longest side in the triangle below.

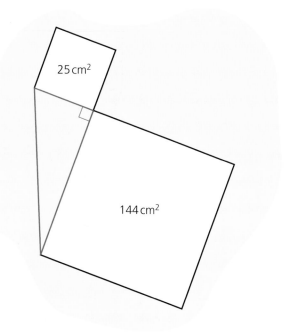

Student's Book exercise 2.1

Work out the length of the side marked *x* in each of the following questions.

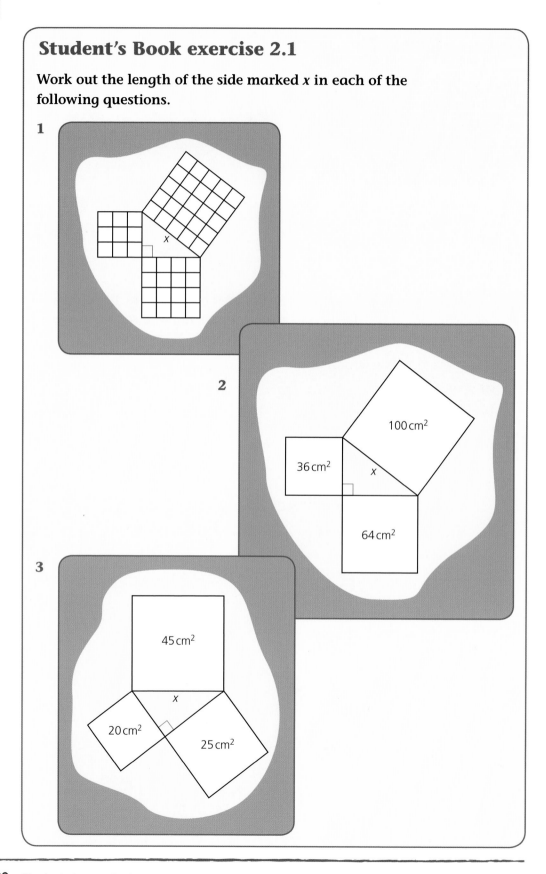

1

2

100 cm²

36 cm²   *x*

64 cm²

3

45 cm²

x

20 cm²

25 cm²

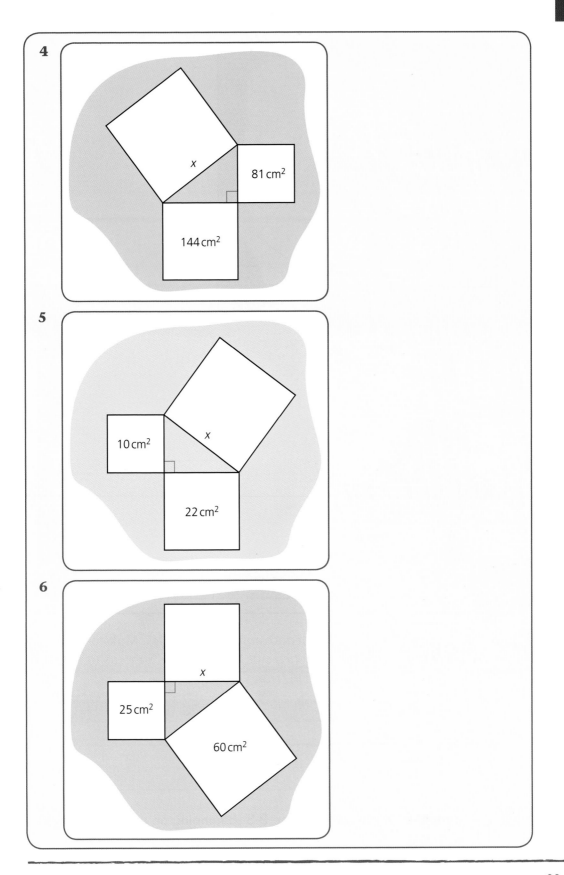

4

x

81 cm²

144 cm²

5

10 cm²

x

22 cm²

6

25 cm²

x

60 cm²

7

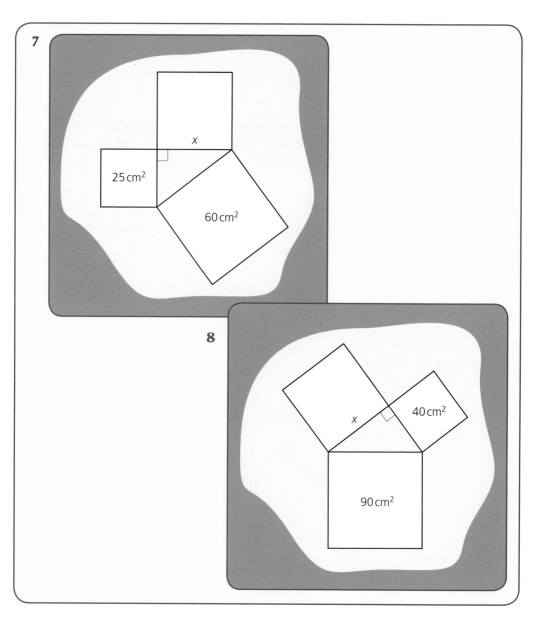

25 cm²

x

60 cm²

8

x

40 cm²

90 cm²

34 The table below shows the side lengths of some triangles. Make a sketch of each one and draw squares on each side. Then use Pythagoras to decide whether or not it is a right-angled triangle.

Lengths of sides of triangle	Is the triangle right-angled?
3 cm, 4 cm, 5 cm	
7 cm, 8 cm, 9 cm	
7 cm, 24 cm, 25 cm	

 Complete Workbook exercise 2.3 (beginning on page 17 of your workbook).

Summary

In this chapter you looked at various types of triangle and were introduced to Pythagoras' rule:

If a triangle is right-angled, then the area of the square on the longest side is the same as the sum of the areas of the squares on the other two sides.

Or in other words:

If the area of the two yellow squares is added together, they will always equal the area of the red square (9 + 16 = 25).

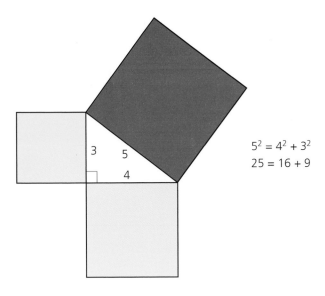

$$5^2 = 4^2 + 3^2$$
$$25 = 16 + 9$$

Counting

1 How many bottles are there in:

   a) a full crate of beer (Damm)?

   b) a box of water?

   c) a crate of Schweppes lemonade?

2 The drawing below shows a crate of bottles with some spaces. How many bottles are there in the crate? Explain exactly how you counted them.

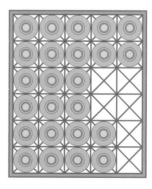

John, Paul, Mary and Jim are discussing how they worked out
the answer to **question 2**.

- John counted 6, then 12, then 18. Then he added 4 more to make 22.
  Then 2 more to make 24.
- Paul counted 5, 10, 13, 16, 20, 24.
- Mary counted 6×5 to make 30 and then subtracted 6.
- Jim rearranged the bottles and then did 4×6 to get 24.

Make sure you understand each of these methods before moving on.

 Now turn to pages 22–23 in your workbook and try Workbook
exercise 3.1.

3 Joe is delivering crates of bottles to the supermarket. There are 30 bottles
in a crate. His trolley will hold four full crates.

How many bottles can fit on Joe's trolley altogether?

4 The supermarket asked for 25 full crates. How many journeys will Joe
have to make with his trolley?

5 Suggest how Joe might stack the 25 crates in the warehouse.

6 How many bottles did the supermarket order altogether?

7 Below are some displays of goods that can be seen at a Spanish market. In each case, write down how many items you think there are in the display. Also write down whether each of your answers is exact or an estimate.

a)

b)

c)

Stacking shelves

8 Pete works at a supermarket after school. His main job is stacking the shelves and making sure they are full.

How many packs of Anchor butter are there on the shelf at the moment?

9 Packs of Anchor butter can be stacked four packs deep and five packs high. How many more packs can he fit on the shelf?

10 The packs of butter in the photo below can be packed five deep and four high. How many packs can fit on the shelf altogether?

11 The manager says to Pete: 'We only have 100 packs and I want the display to look as full as possible.' How would you advise Pete to stack the butter in order to satisfy the manager?

Now try the questions in Workbook exercise 3.2 (beginning on page 24 of your workbook).

Packing cubes

12 The drawings below show some arrangements of centimetre cubes
(sometimes written as cm³).

For each of the pictures, write down how many cubes there are. Write a
sentence for each about how you counted the cubes.

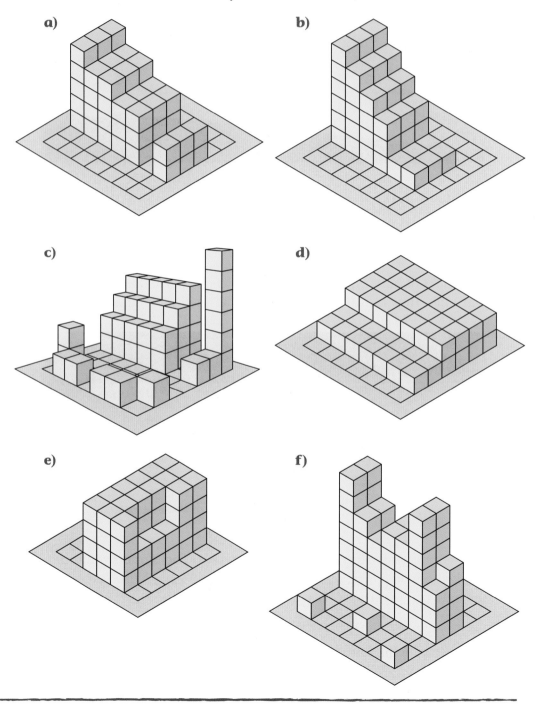

a)

b)

c)

d)

e)

f)

13 The cubes in **question 12a)** are to be put in the box on the right. The internal dimensions of the box are 5 cm by 3 cm by 4 cm. The box has a lid on it.

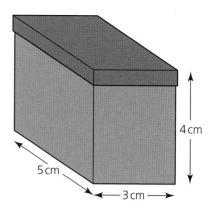

John says: 'I don't think that all the cubes will fit in the box.'

To see if he is right, he first of all gets enough cubes to fill the bottom of the box.

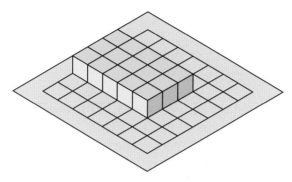

He then rearranges all the cubes like this to show what he means.

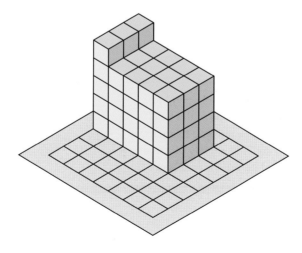

Is John right? How many cubes won't fit into the box?

14 Jane says: 'I started like this when I filled the box.'

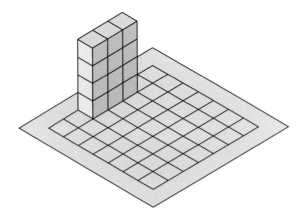

How many arrangements of this kind will Jane need to fill the box? How many cubes will she have left over?

15 For each of the drawings in **questions 12b)**, **c)**, **d)** and **e)**, say whether or not the cubes will fit into a 5 × 3 × 4 cm box. Say whether or not there would be any space left, or whether there would be any cubes left over. In each case make a drawing to show how you would start to fill the box.

16 The cubes in **question 12f)** are to be put into a box that measures 7 × 2 × 5 cm. Will these cubes fit exactly into the box, or will there be some left over?

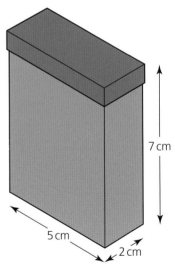

7 cm

5 cm

2 cm

> The number of cm cubes that can fit into a box is called the **volume** of the box. For example, the box that you used in **questions 13–15** could fit exactly 60 cubes in it. We say that its volume is 60 cm³.

17 The picture below shows how we could fill the box used in **question 16**.

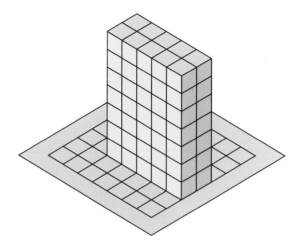

What is the volume of this box?

18 Below is another box that we want to fill with cm cubes. What is the volume of this box?

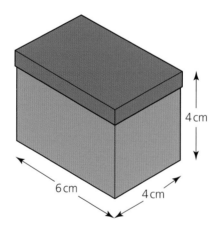

4 cm

6 cm

4 cm

19 Make a drawing to show how you would fill this box with cm cubes.

 Now try Workbook exercise 3.3 on page 26 of your workbook.

At the cheese counter

Mariam serves on the cheese counter of a supermarket. One of her jobs is to cut cheese into 1 cm cubes and then pack them.

20 Mariam begins with the block of cheese shown here. She wants to cut it into 1 cm cubes. The block is 4 cm high.

Make a drawing to show how Mariam would cut the block into 1 cm cubes. Then write down the volume of the block.

Mariam also has to cut, pack and price various different cuts of cheese.

21 She begins with a new block of cheese as shown here. It is a cuboid measuring 10 cm × 8 cm × 4 cm. This piece of cheese is priced at £2.40.

Below are some of the pieces she cuts. For each one, write down the price that you think Mariam should charge. The height of each piece is still 4 cm.

a)

b)

c)

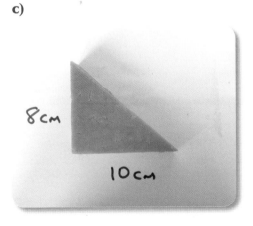

d)

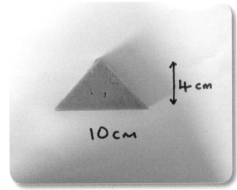

22 Mariam also cuts some pieces as shown.

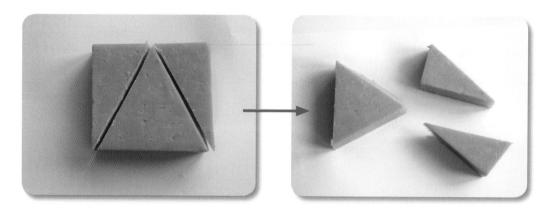

She puts a price of £1.20 onto the larger piece. She puts prices of £0.60 onto each of the smaller pieces. Is Mariam right to do this? Use a drawing to help you explain your answer.

23 Look again at the solids in **question 21**. All of these solids have mathematical names. For each of the five solids, write down the names that describe them. Some may have more than one name. Choose from the options below.

> **cube   triangle   cuboid   rectangle   rectangular prism**
>
> **square   triangular prism**

24 In **question 20** you worked out that the volume of the original block of cheese was 320 cm³. What are the volumes of the pieces of cheese shown in **question 21**?

25 Mariam is asked to make a display by combining blocks of cheese. She decides to use two of the blocks shown opposite.

The first combination looks like this:

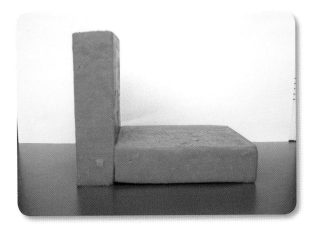

Work out the total volume of this shape.

26 She then uses a different block to get a display like this:

If the display is 10 cm high:

a) Work out the volume of the orange block.

b) Work out the volume of the yellow block.

c) Work out the total volume of the display.

27 For another display, Mariam just sketches a couple of ideas about what it will look like.

Work out the total volume of cheese needed for each display.

Display 1

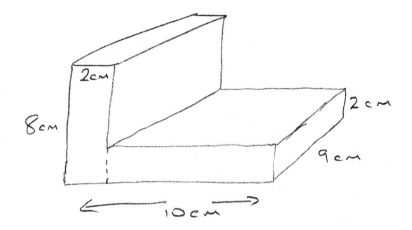

Display 2

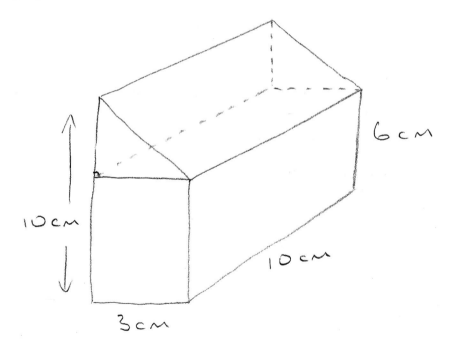

The chocolate counter

28 In the chocolate section a new product is on sale.

The Biarritz chocolate box has a base of 20 cm, a height of 10 cm, and a depth of 1 cm.

What is the volume of one chocolate box?

29 If a display consists of 10 of these boxes, what would be the total volume of the display?

Finding volumes

30 Cain was given the following homework questions by his teacher:

1 Draw a sketch of a box (cuboid) that measures 6 cm × 5 cm × 8 cm. Show how you would fill this box with cm cubes. Use this to write down the volume of the box.

2 The drawing shows a box in the shape of a triangular prism. Show how you would work out the volume of the box.

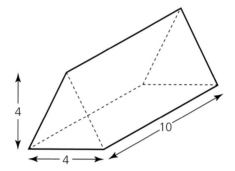

3 The following shape is made from two cuboids. Work out its volume. Use a drawing to show how you worked it out.

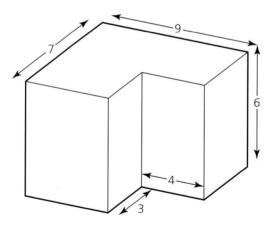

When the teacher collected the homework, she found that Cain had started every question, but hadn't finished any of them (he's better at drawing than he is at maths!).

His answers are shown in **Workbook exercise 3.4**, which begins on page 27 of your workbook.

For each question, finish what Cain started and fully answer the question.

Student's Book exercise 3.1

Find the volumes of the following shapes.

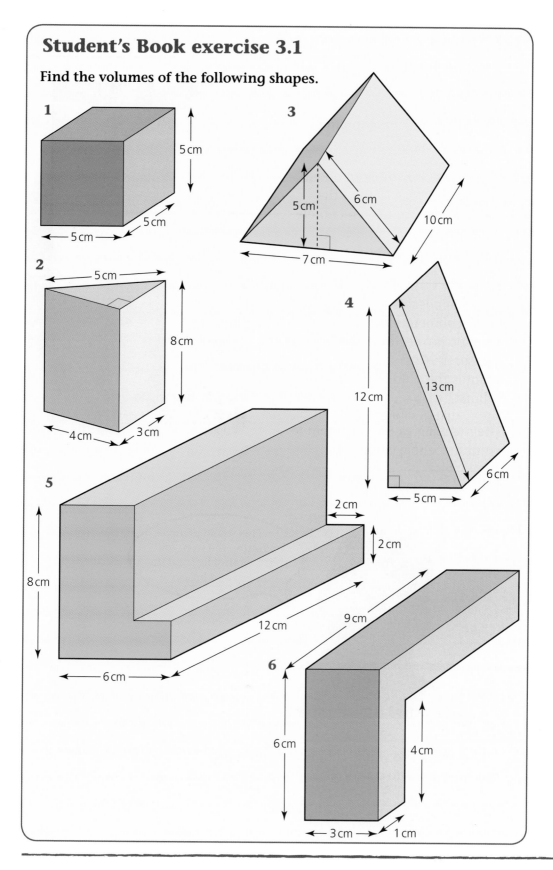

1 5 cm, 5 cm, 5 cm

2 5 cm, 8 cm, 4 cm, 3 cm

3 5 cm, 6 cm, 7 cm, 10 cm

4 12 cm, 13 cm, 5 cm, 6 cm

5 8 cm, 6 cm, 12 cm, 2 cm, 2 cm

6 9 cm, 6 cm, 4 cm, 3 cm, 1 cm

In school

31 As part of an art project, Pete and Fiona are making a display of old cabinets. They are going to paint the cabinet shown here.

Originally, they thought about just painting the front of the cabinet. The front is a rectangle that measures 90 cm × 40 cm. What is the area of the front of the cabinet?

32 They then decide to paint one side of the cabinet as well.
The side is a rectangle that measures 90 cm × 50 cm.
What is the area of the side of the cabinet?

33 Their teacher would like them to paint the whole cabinet.

Pete says:

> This would mean painting the front and back, both sides, and the top and base.

If they paint the whole cabinet, including the base, what is the total area that they have to paint?

34 This computer cabinet is a cuboid. The top measures 50 cm by 50 cm and it is 80 cm high.

a) If Fiona wanted to paint one side of this cabinet, what area would she have to paint?

b) Fiona decides to paint the whole cabinet, including the base. What is the total area she has to paint?

> The total area Fiona has to paint is called the **surface area** of the solid.

Student's Book exercise 3.2

Work out the surface areas of the following shapes.

1

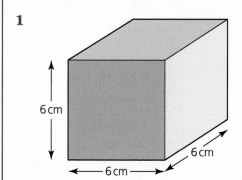

6 cm
6 cm
6 cm

2

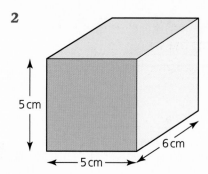

5 cm
5 cm
6 cm

3

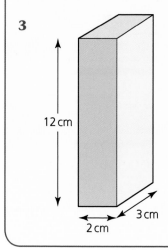

12 cm
3 cm
2 cm

35 For another cuboid, Pete worked out the total surface area. He used the following calculation:

$(5 \times 4) \times 2 + (5 \times 7) \times 2 + (4 \times 7) \times 2$

Draw the cuboid that Pete was working on.

 Now try Workbook exercise 3.5 on page 29 of your workbook.

Student's Book exercise 3.3

Work out the surface area of the following shapes.

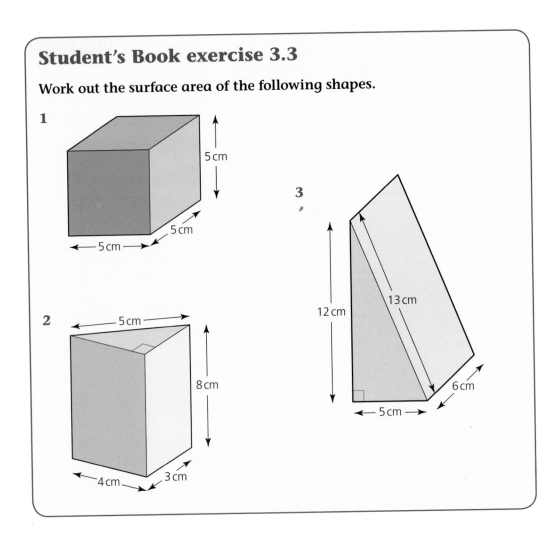

1

5 cm
5 cm
5 cm

2

5 cm
8 cm
4 cm
3 cm

3

12 cm
13 cm
5 cm
6 cm

Summary

This chapter has been concerned with finding the **volume** and **surface area** of 3-D shapes.

The **volume** is the number of cm cubes that will fit into the shape.

The **surface area** is the total area we would have to paint if we painted all the faces of the shape.

To find the volume of a cuboid, we would usually begin with either a layer on the base of the shape like this:

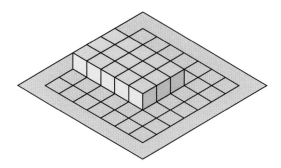

Or a vertical layer like this:

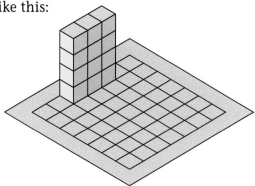

We would then keep repeating the layers until it was full.

So this cuboid has a volume of 60 cm³.

To find the **surface area** of a shape, we add up the areas of all the faces. The faces will always either be rectangles or triangles.

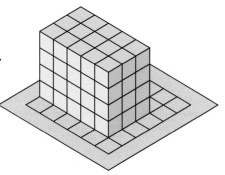

The total surface area of the cuboid is 20 + 20 + 12 + 12 + 15 + 15 = 94 cm²

Sometimes we slice a cuboid in half to make triangular prisms. To find the volume of a triangular prism, we work out how many cm cubes would fit into the cuboid and then halve that number.

So, for example, the triangular prism below can be seen as half of a 12 × 5 × 6 cuboid.

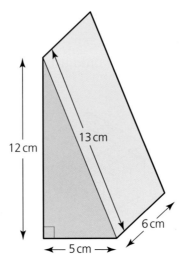

The volume of the cuboid would be 360 cm³, and so the volume of the triangular prism is 180 cm³.

A stitch in time

1 Lin has her own company making designer t-shirts. Her latest design includes coloured circles of fabric. These will be hand-stitched with sequins as shown in the picture. They will then be sewn onto the t-shirt.

To decide on a price for her t-shirts, Lin must estimate how long it will take her to sew the sequins onto each circle.

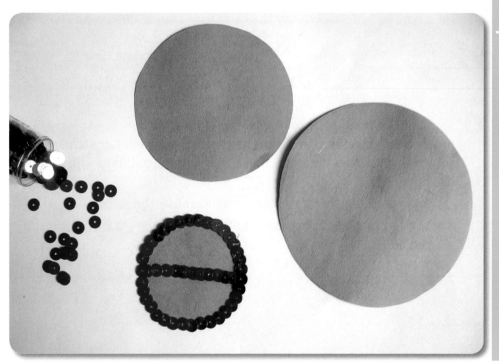

For the smallest circle it took Lin 2 minutes and 20 seconds to sew the line of sequins across the middle.

Estimate how long it will take her to sew the sequins around the edge of this circle. Explain how you made your estimate.

2 For the middle-sized circle it took Lin 3 minutes and 30 seconds to sew the line of sequins across the middle.

Estimate how long it will take her to sew the sequins around the edge of this circle. Explain your method.

3 How long do you think it will take Lin to sew all the sequins on the largest circle shown in the photo on the previous page? The design will be the same as for the other two circles, with a row of sequins across the middle and around the edge. Say how you made your estimate.

Turn to pages 30–31 in your workbook and answer the questions in Workbook exercise 4.1.

4 Some of Lin's designs use beads. Lin wants to know how many beads to order so she has enough for all her t-shirts. To help her estimate she lays some beads across the middle of her design and makes some marks on it, as shown here.

a) Say what you think she has done to make the marks.

b) Use her method to estimate how many beads would go around the edge.

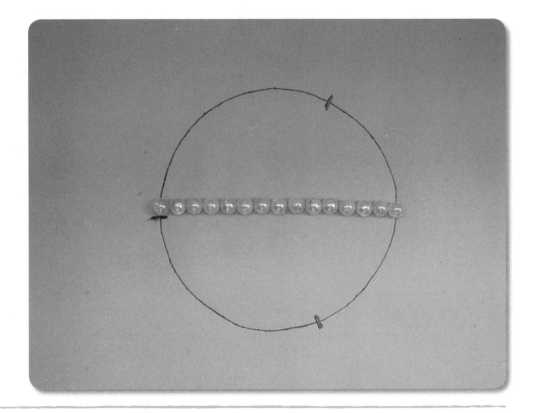

5 In some cases Lin does not have enough beads to place across the middle. Instead she measures the length of one bead and the diameter of the circle. Her drawings are shown below.

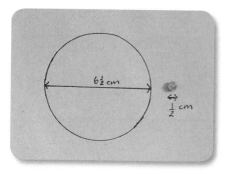

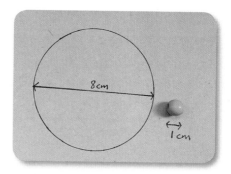

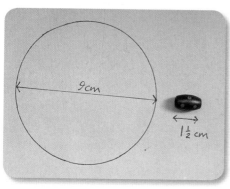

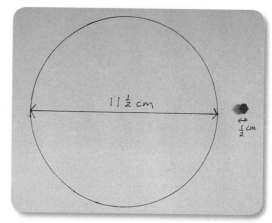

a) Which of the designs do you think will need the most beads? Explain your thinking. (Remember that the design has beads across the middle **and** around the edge.)

b) Work out roughly how many beads will be needed in total for each design.

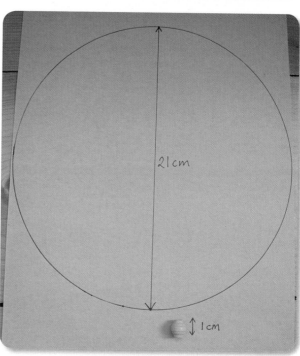

The swimming circuit

6 The picture shows a circular pool. On average it takes Caroline 2 minutes to swim one circuit around the edge of the pool.

Estimate how long you think it would take her to swim in a straight line across the middle of the pool from one side to the other.

7 a) Use compasses to make accurate drawings of the following:

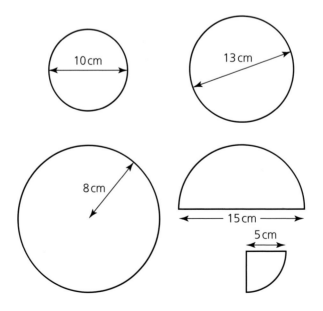

b) Estimate the distance around each of the diagrams you have drawn.

Touching the circle 1

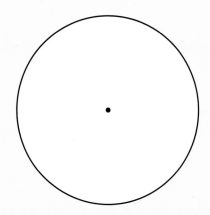

Look at the circle above.
- Where do you see the diameter in this picture?
- Where else can you see the diameter?
- Where else can you see the diameter?
- Run your finger along all the places you can see a diameter.
- Where do you see the radius in this picture?
- Run your finger along all the places you can see the radius.
- Where do you see the circumference in this picture?
- Where else can you see the circumference?

Indicate with your finger where you can see:
- the diameter
- the radius } in the circumference

The circle: Using formulas

8 This is a very well-known formula in maths:

> **Circumference = π × diameter**

Describe in a few sentences how you think this formula relates to the work you've been doing on circles.

9 This is another well-known formula in maths:

> **Circumference = 2 × π × radius**

Antonia says: 'I don't understand this formula. If the question tells me the radius of the circle then I just double that and times it by roughly 3 (3.14) to work out the circumference.'

How is Antonia's method the same as doing 2 × π × radius?
How is it different?

Mirrors

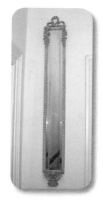

10 Imagine that you are making the mirrors shown in the photos above.

   a) Which parts would take the most work?

   b) Which of the three mirrors do you think would cost the most to make?

11 Below are designs for two other mirrors. Both are edged in wood. The circular wooden edging costs £7 per foot. The straight wooden edging costs £4 per foot.

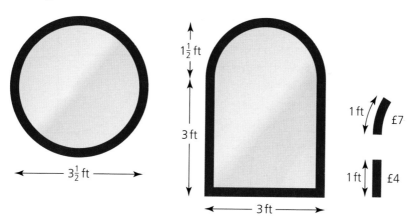

   a) Which of the two mirrors has the largest viewing area? Explain how you know.

   b) Which of the two designs would cost the most to edge in wood?

   c) What happens if you use π in your calculations for part **b)**? How does this affect the difference in the cost of the two edges?

Turn to pages 32–33 in your workbook and answer the questions in Workbook exercise 4.2.

The trampoline

12 Tony and Lin's children no longer use the trampoline in their garden. Underneath the trampoline is a circle of grass that is very bare. Once the trampoline has gone, Tony decides to re-turf the bare area. He is not sure how much turf he will need. He asks the man at the garden centre for advice.

The man at the garden centre draws this picture.

He tells Tony to buy enough turf to fill the three squares. He says that's roughly the amount needed to cover the circle. Tony isn't sure about this.

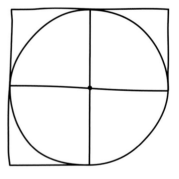

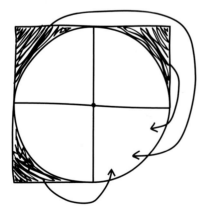

The man adds to his picture like this. He says that you can use the bits round the edge to fill in the missing part.

Tony still isn't sure that this will work.

a) Sketch or trace the first picture.

b) Will buying enough turf to cover the three squares be enough to cover the whole circle? Move the shaded pieces to help you decide.

At home Tony measures from the middle to the edge of the trampoline. It is 6 feet. He then draws a more accurate picture as shown.

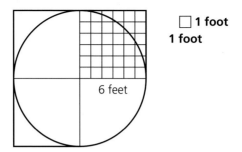

c) How many squares of turf (1 foot by 1 foot) will be needed for the three large squares?

d) Roughly how many squares of turf will be needed for the whole circle?

e) Will Tony have the right amount of turf if he buys enough for three large squares? What would you advise him to do?

13 Tony's neighbour Brendan is also getting rid of his trampoline. He has the same problem with his grass. He asks Tony how much turf he should buy. Tony describes the method of drawing on the large squares and using that as a guide.

Brendan's trampoline measures 8 feet from the middle to the edge. How many squares of turf (1 foot by 1 foot) would you advise him to buy? Draw a picture to help you decide.

Turn to pages 34–35 in your workbook and answer the questions in Workbook exercise 4.3.

14 Turf is sold in different-sized pieces. The machines which cut the turf are still set in imperial measurements which is why all the measurements are given in feet.

Work out an approximate cost for turfing the following areas.

£3 ─ ☐ 4 feet
4 feet

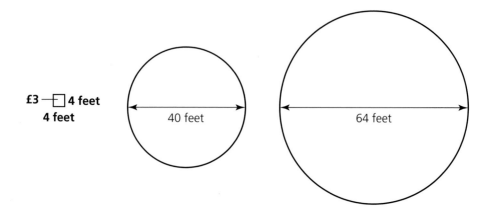

40 feet

64 feet

Turn to pages 36–37 in your workbook and answer the questions in Workbook exercise 4.4.

Touching the circle 2

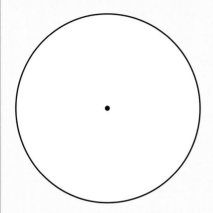

Look at the circle above.

- Where do you see the radius in this picture?
- Run your finger along all the places you can see the radius.
- Where can you see the radius × radius in this picture?
- Describe some other places where you can see the radius × radius in this picture.
- Where do you see three lots of radius × radius in this picture?

The formula shown in the box is a well-known formula in maths.

> **Area of a circle = π × radius²   π ≈ 3.14**

Where can you see the area in the picture above?

Where can you see radius² in the picture above?

Where can you see π in the picture above?

Mirrors and circles

15 Find the area in squares units of the following shapes in two ways:

  a) using your method of estimating

  b) using the rule: area $= \pi r^2$

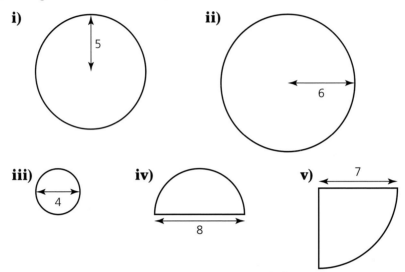

i) 5

ii) 6

iii) 4

iv) 8

v) 7

  c) For each shape compare your answer for part **a)** with your answer for part **b)**. Which answer gives you a better idea of the area of the shape? Explain.

16 a) Look again at these mirrors and decide which one has the biggest viewing area.

$3\frac{1}{2}$ ft

$1\frac{1}{2}$ ft

3 ft

3 ft

  b) Use the rule: area $= \pi r^2$ to accurately find the areas of the two mirrors.

  c) Were you right with your prediction in part **a)**?

Turn to pages 38–39 in your workbook and answer the questions in Workbook exercise 4.5.

Summary

In this chapter you have looked at how the diameter and the circumference of a circle relate to each other. This can be seen in the diagram below:

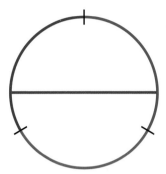

You also looked at how the area of a square drawn on the radius relates to the area of a circle.

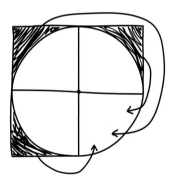

In other words you looked at the meaning behind the formula for the circumfrence of a circle:

$$C = \pi \times d$$

You also looked at the meaning behind the formula for the area of a circle:

$$A = \pi \times r^2$$

Tiles within tiles

1 This picture shows a room with a tiled floor. Each tile is about 50 cm by 50 cm. The room is 3 m by 3 m.

a) With your hands show the approximate size of one tile.

b) Roughly mark out the size of the 3 m by 3 m room in your classroom.

c) How many tiles were needed to tile the room? Talk to a partner about how you worked this out.

2 a) Maria wants to re-tile the room using 25 cm by 25 cm tiles. She says: 'I will need twice as many tiles as before.' Can you explain her thinking and why she is wrong?

b) How many tiles do you think she will need?

c) Michael said: 'I worked it out by imagining how many tiles fitted along one edge of the room. Then I imagined gradually filling the floor with rows of tiles.' **Workbook exercise 5.1** (page 40) in your workbook has a grid that shows a plan of the original tiles in the room. Using this grid show how Michael worked out the number of tiles.

3 Gareth said he had a different way of seeing it. He cut out a piece of card and put it on top of one of the original tiles as shown in this picture.

He said: 'You can tell how many of the new tiles will fit on an old one. This lets you work out how many you need altogether.'

Discuss this approach in pairs. Can you see Gareth's approach using the drawing you did for Michael's approach in **question 2c)**?

4 Each larger tile costs £28 and each smaller tile costs £8. Is it more expensive to tile the room using smaller or larger tiles? Explain your answer.

Now turn to Workbook exercise 5.2 (which begins on page 41 of your workbook) and try these two approaches with several other types of tile.

Playground

5 The picture shows a playground in a primary school. As you can see, most of the playground is taken up by a five-a-side football pitch.

a) Most of the children are 10 years old. How tall do you think they are?

b) Estimate the diameter of the goalkeeper's area.

c) Estimate the radius of the centre circle.

d) How tall do you think the goal is?

e) Estimate the dimensions of the football pitch.

6 The picture below shows a close-up view of the paving used on the pitch.

    a) Estimate the size of each slab.

    b) How many slabs are needed to pave the whole pitch?

7 The school has decided to build another pitch of the same size. They could use these slabs again, which are £2.50 each. Alternatively they could use slabs of twice the size (i.e. each side is twice as long), which are £8 each. Which would be cheaper? Compare your method with others in your class.

Student's Book exercise 5.1

1 A square has an area of 24 m². What is the area of a square with dimensions that are half this?

2 a) A rectangle has dimensions of 3 m by 5 m. What is its area?

    b) Another rectangle has dimensions of 6 m by 10 m. Explain, using a drawing, why the larger rectangle has an area four times bigger than the smaller rectangle.

3 A room has floor dimensions of 3 m by 5 m. How many 50 cm by 50 cm tiles will be needed to tile the floor? Explain why you'd need four times as many 25 cm by 25 cm tiles to tile the room.

4 A basketball court is usually 28 m long by 15 m wide. Special wooden floor blocks are used to cover the court.

    a) How many blocks of 28 cm by 15 cm will be needed?

    b) If the blocks were 56 cm by 30 cm how many would you need?

8 The cuboid above is made of cubes that are 2 cm by 2 cm by 2 cm.

a) How many cubes does it take to make the cuboid?

b) If you used cubes that are 1 cm by 1 cm by 1 cm to make this same cuboid, how many would you need? It may help to look at the picture below.

9 a) What are the dimensions of this cuboid? (The cubes on the far right of the cuboid are 1 cm by 1 cm by 1 cm cubes.)

b) How many 1 cm by 1 cm by 1 cm cubes would you see if you were looking at the face of the cuboid from the right (in the direction shown by the arrow)?

c) What is the volume of this cuboid? Is your method similar to Michael's method from **question 2c)**?

d) What is the volume of a cube that is 2 cm by 2 cm by 2 cm?

Student's Book exercise 5.2

1 This cuboid is three bricks high, five bricks long and four bricks deep. Each brick is 2 cm by 2 cm by 2 cm.

a) Using the picture, work out how many cubes are needed to make the cuboid.

b) Work out its volume.

c) Now use a different method to find the volume.

2 A cuboid is two bricks high, three bricks deep and four bricks long. Each brick is 3 cm by 3 cm by 3 cm. What is its volume?

3 A modern art display is made from 36 cubes that are each 2 cm by 2 cm by 2 cm. What is the volume of the cubes used?

4 The volume of a cuboid is 135 cm³. Give a possible example of the dimensions of this cuboid. How many 3 cm by 3 cm by 3 cm cubes would be needed to make it?

5 What is the volume of a cuboid made from 8 3 cm by 3 cm by 3 cm cubes?

6 If you have a cube made from 64 1 cm³ cubes, what do you think its dimensions are?

Orange juice

10 The picture below shows a 1 litre carton of orange juice and a Perspex cube with internal dimensions of 10 cm by 10 cm by 10 cm.

a) What is the internal volume of the cube?

b) Roughly how many pints are there in a litre?

c) If you pour the orange juice into the Perspex cube, do you think it will overflow, just fill it, or only partially fill it? Explain your ideas to a partner.

> A litre exactly fills a 10 cm by 10 cm by 10 cm cube.
> This means that a litre is exactly 1000 cm cubes (1000 cm³).

11 a) This picture shows a Perspex cube of 20 cm by 20 cm by 20 cm. It is next to a cube of 10 cm by 10 cm by 10 cm. If you pour the orange juice from the small cube into the large cube, how far up do you think it will go? Explain your reasoning.

b) How many litres of orange juice would fit into this large cube?

Student's Book exercise 5.3

1 Put the containers in the above picture in order of size. The Perspex cube is the same as the one used in **question 10**.

2 What is the volume of a 2 litre bottle of cola in cm³?

3 What is the volume of a 1½ litre bottle of water in cm³?

4 A can of lemonade is about 330 cm³. What is this in litres?
How many cans of lemonade would it take to fill the Perspex cube in the pictures below?

5 A pint glass holds about half a litre.

   a) Roughly how many pints of cola would you get from a 2 litre bottle?

   b) Roughly how many pints of water would you get from a 1½ litre bottle of water?

   c) Roughly how far up the pint glass would the lemonade from a 330 cm³ can reach?

6 A cuboid-shaped container has dimensions of 20 cm by 10 cm by 10 cm. How much water could it hold in litres?

7 Draw a sketch to help you answer the following:

   a) How many 1 cm² squares fit into 1 m²?

   b) How many 1 cm³ cubes fit into 1 m³?

There are 12 inches in a foot.

8 What is 1 ft² in square inches?

9 What is 1 ft³ in cubic inches?

10 A cuboid is made from 2 cm cubes. There are 24 cubes altogether. What is the volume of the cuboid in cm³?

Wooden blocks

Student's Book exercise 5.4

1 The picture shows four blue wooden cubes and four flat blue cuboids. Each cube is 1 inch by 1 inch by 1 inch. The volume of one cube is 1 cubic inch.

Estimate the dimensions of the flat blue cuboids above.

2 What is the surface area of one cube? What is the surface area of one cuboid?

3 This picture shows the same blue cubes.

Estimate the volume and surface area of each of the other objects in the picture.

Summary

This chapter has focused on working out how many smaller tiles or cubes fit into a larger tile or cube.

Two ways of doing this have been explored:

- Find out how many smaller tiles or cubes fit into a row or layer. Then find out how many rows or layers there are.

- If you already know how many tiles or cubes of one type are needed, then you only need to find out how many of the new tiles or cubes fit into one of the old tiles or cubes.